Journeys

Paul Mason

Heinemann Library
Chicago, Illinois

© 2004 Heinemann Library
a division of Reed Elsevier Inc.
Chicago, Illinois

Customer Service 888-454-2279
Visit our website at www.heinemannlibrary.com

Designed by David Poole and Geoff Ward
Originated by Ambassador Litho Ltd
Printed in China by Wing King Tong

08 07 06 05 04
10 9 8 7 6 5 4 3 2 1

**Library of Congress Cataloging-in-Publication
Data**
Mason, Paul, 1967-
  Journeys / Paul Mason.
      p. cm. -- (Rites of passage)
Summary: Explains the origin, historical or religious
significance, and practice of different types of journeys in
various cultures around the world.
Includes bibliographical references and index.
  ISBN 1-4034-3988-5 (lib. bdg.) -- ISBN 1-4034-2513-2
(pbk.)
  1. Voyages and travels--Juvenile literature. 2. Pilgrims
and pilgrimages--Juvenile literature. [1. Voyages and
travels. 2. Pilgrims and pilgrimages. 3. Rites and
ceremonies.] I. Title. II. Series.
GT5220.M37 2003
  910--dc21
                    2003001898

Acknowledgments
The author and publisher are grateful to the following
for permission to reproduce copyright material:
Cover photograph: Getty Images/Nabeel Turner.
p. 4 Gavriel Jecan/Corbis; p. 5 David Samuel
Robbins/Corbis; p. 6 Carmen Redondo/Corbis; pp. 7, 12
Hanan Isachar/ Corbis; p. 9 Nik Wheeler/Corbis; p. 10
Chris Bland/Corbis/Eye Ubiquitous; p. 11 Jacques M.
Chenet/Corbis; p. 13 James Marshall/Corbis; p. 14 Mary
Evans; p. 15 Robert Harding/ Photri Inc; p. 16 Albrecht G.
Schaefer/Corbis; p. 17 Roman Soumar/Corbis; p. 18
Bennett Dean/Corbis/Eye Ubiquitous; p. 19 Daniel
O'Leary/Panos; p. 20 Nabeel Turner/Getty Images; p. 21
Magnum/Abbas; p. 22 Jirina Simajchlova/Tibet Images;
pp. 23, 27 Galen Rowell/Corbis; p. 24 Abbie Enock/ Travel
Ink; p. 25 L. Clarke/Corbis; p. 26 Michael St. Maur
Sheil/Corbis; p. 28 Derek Croucher/Corbis; p. 29 Steve
McCurry/Magnum.

Special thanks to both the Interfaith Education Center in
Bradford, England, and Georga Godwin for their help in
the preparation of this book.

Every effort has been made to contact copyright holders
of any material reproduced in this book. Any omissions
will be rectified in subsequent printings if notice is given
to the publishers.

Some words are shown in
bold, **like this.** You can find out
what they mean by looking in
the glossary.

Contents

Special Journeys

There are many different kinds of journeys. Most journeys are very ordinary. When you go to the supermarket in the car, for example, there is probably nothing special about the trip. Some journeys, though, are special. This book is about these special journeys and the reasons people make them.

Religious journeys

Some journeys are special because they are an important part of a religion. They are called **pilgrimages.** Some people go on a pilgrimage because it is their religious duty. **Muslims,** for example, are supposed to visit their most **holy** city, Mecca, at least once in their life if possible.

On many pilgrimages, the journey itself is as important as the place where it ends. Tibetan **Buddhists** in China follow certain routes on their pilgrimages that take them to various holy places, for example. So do **Christian** pilgrims visiting Santiago de Compostela in Spain.

Pilgrims bathe in the Ganges River. Many have journeyed hundreds of miles to get there.

Other journeys

Other special journeys are not linked to religion at all. For example, in 1911, the explorer Robert F. Scott set off with a team of men to try to reach the South Pole. They hoped to be the first people to get there. Scott's attempt to be first to the Pole failed and he and his men died, but they became a **symbol** of the spirit of bravery and exploration.

These flags in the Himalayan mountains have prayers written on them. People believe the wind carries the prayers to heaven.

Rites of passage

In 1909, Arnold van Gennep wrote about rites of passage. He made up this term to mean events that mark important times in a person's life. He said there are three changes in every rite of passage:

- leaving one group,
- moving on to a new stage,
- and joining a new group.

Bible Journeys

The **Christian** Bible tells of many journeys. Among the most important are those leading up to the birth of Jesus in Bethlehem.

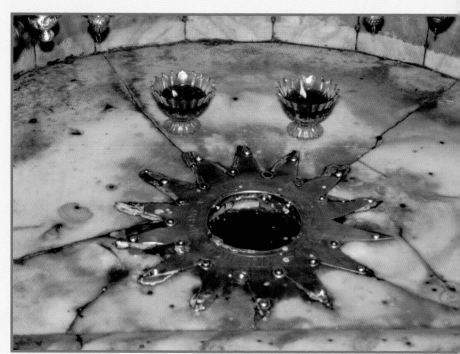

This close-up shows part of the site of the Nativity in Bethlehem, Israel, where Jesus is believed to have been born.

Mary and Joseph

One of the first journey stories in the **New Testament** tells of the arrival of Mary and Joseph, Jesus's parents. They had to travel to Bethlehem to be counted in a population count. When they arrived, it was impossible to find a place to stay for the night. Mary and Joseph ended up sleeping in a stable with the animals. This stable is where Jesus was born.

Today, many **Christians** visit Bethlehem, especially at Christmas, which marks the birth of Jesus. They go there to remember this important birth. One of the most popular places to visit is the Church of the Nativity. It stands in the spot were Jesus is thought to have been born. A **mass** is said outside at midnight, and the area is always full of people.

The wise men and the shepherds

Another story tells of a group of shepherds that arrived soon after Jesus' birth. They had been told to come by an angel. They had traveled down from their flocks of sheep in the hills to welcome the Son of God to Earth. Kings from far away also came to bring gifts for the newborn baby, Jesus.

Today, many Christian travelers visit the Shepherds' Fields, where the angel is said to have appeared. People visit all year, but the site is especially popular at Christmas.

This photo shows a procession *of Greek Orthodox Christians at Christmastime in Bethlehem.*

Sarah's story

Sarah, now eleven years old, remembers her visit to Shepherds' Fields:

I went to Shepherds' Fields with my family when I was five. It was Christmastime, and I remember feeling amazed. I was standing there in the very spot where an angel appeared to the shepherds. There were loads of other people there too, but it was still easy to imagine.

The Way of Saint James

One of the oldest **pilgrim** routes in Europe is the *Camino de Santiago*—Spanish for the "Way of Saint James." The ancient path ends at the Spanish city of Santiago de Compostela. This city is where the remains of Saint James, one of the twelve **apostles,** are said to lie.

The journey to Santiago first became popular more than 1,000 years ago. The Bishop of Le Puy, in France, was one of the first to make the trip in 950 C.E. People went to Santiago to see and touch the bones of the saint. They believed that the saint would help them speak to God and ask forgiveness for their **sins.** Today, the journey has become a celebration for many **Christians.**

The Camino de Santiago is said to start at Saint-Jean-Pied-de-Port and end at Santiago. Many routes from across Europe lead pilgrims toward the start of the path.

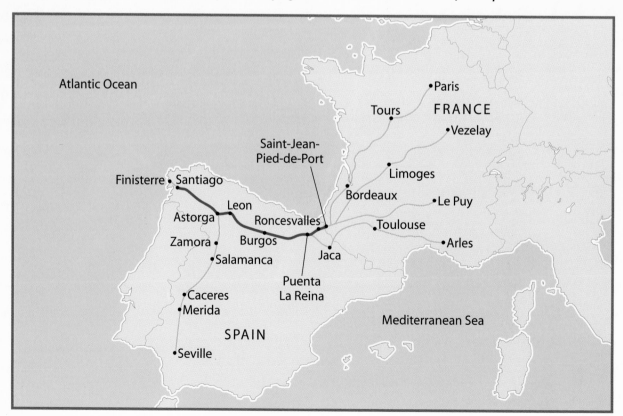

These pilgrims on the Way of Saint James are moving forward on their knees. The way of Saint James must be walked the entire way.

The Way of Saint James winds 480 miles (800 kilometers) from the foothills of the Pyrenees Mountains to Santiago. Most people begin their journey at Roncesvalles, France. There are places for pilgrims to rest along the way. It takes most people a month to complete the journey.

Evelyn's story

Evelyn Lapasset walked part of the Way of Saint James when she was fourteen years old:

I walked the route in two parts, the second part one year after the first. We began in Saint-Jean-Pied-de-Port the first year and finished in Burgos. It was very hard, but fun to meet all the other people on the journey.

Christian Journeys

Every year, hundreds of thousands of **Christians** visit the Holy Land. This area of land is mainly in Israel, at the eastern edge of the Mediterranean Sea. **Jews** and **Muslims** also visit the Holy Land because many of their **holy** sites are in this area, too.

One of the most popular places for Christians to visit is the city of Jerusalem, where Jesus preached many of his lessons. Many Christians visit the Praetorium, the building where Jesus was tried and found guilty of **treason** against Rome—which ruled over the area at the time. They may also follow Jesus' route through the streets as he carried the cross to the place where he was **crucified.**

Lourdes

Each year about three million Christians travel to Lourdes, France. They go there mainly because they hope to be cured of sicknesses. Christians have visited the town since 1858. In that year, a fourteen-year-old girl named Bernadette Soubirous had a number of visions of the **Virgin Mary** in a grotto (small cave) nearby. The young girl was later made a saint.

This chapel at Lourdes was built because of the miracles that Christians believe happened there. Today, many people journey to the chapel, in hopes that they will be cured of sickness.

Pope John Paul II became Pope in 1978. He visits many countries so that Catholics around the world who can not afford to visit the Vatican in Italy can see him.

Rome

Another popular place of **pilgrimage** for Christians is Rome, Italy. The Roman Catholic Church has its headquarters there, in Vatican City. The head of the Catholic Church is the Pope, who is thought to be God's representative on Earth. People gather in Rome to hear the Pope say **Mass** from a balcony at the Vatican.

Walsingham pilgrimage

There is a legend that in 1061, in Walsingham, England, a woman named Richeldis de Faverches had a three visions. In the visions, Mary took her to the house in Nazareth where the angel Gabriel announced the news of the birth of Jesus. De Faverches was told by Mary to build an exact copy of that house in Walsingham, which she did. The house de Faverches built became the site of pilgrimages for Christians. Many people still visit the house each year.

The Western Wall

One of the world's most-visited **pilgrim** sites is a 2,000-year-old section of wall. Known as the Western Wall, it lies in the Old City of Jerusalem in Israel. Although it is important to many religions, including **Christianity,** it is an especially important place for **Jewish** people. The wall was built to surround the Jew's **holy** Temple. The wall is about 160 feet (49 meters) long and about 40 feet (12 meters) high.

The Western Wall is nearly all that is left of the Temple. It is the most important holy place in Judaism. Jews believe that the rebuilding of the Temple will be one of the signs that the **Messiah** has come.

This model shows the holy Temple of Jerusalem before its destruction by Roman forces in 70 C.E.

This pilgrim visiting the Western Wall is a rabbi (Jewish religious leader) who has journeyed all the way from South Africa.

Each year many Jews visit the Western Wall to say prayers. Some even push their written prayers into holes in the wall. They believe that these prayers have a better chance of being answered by God.

Daniel's story

Thirteen-year-old Daniel Gamon visited the Western Wall with his father in July 2002:

It was amazing to see, knowing that it had been there for two thousand years. What was even more exciting was that while we were there, the Wall began to leak. People told us that when the Western Wall leaks, it's a sign that the Messiah is coming.

We saw lots of other places in Jerusalem, but the Wall was the best. Even hearing that the damp patch might have been caused by a leaking pipe didn't spoil it!

Passover

Passover, also called Pesah (pey-sa), is an annual seven- or eight-day holiday celebrated by **Jewish** people. (It lasts seven days in Israel, and usually eight days elsewhere.) The holiday—which is known as a **pilgrim** festival—remembers the time about 3,000 years ago when the Jews made a great journey. At this time, the Jews were slaves of the Egyptian pharaoh, or king. Moses, a Jewish leader, asked the pharaoh to free the Jews. Finally, after God had sent ten terrible **plagues** to the Egyptians, the pharaoh agreed. The Jews left so suddenly that they did not have time to let their bread dough rise for their journey. Instead, they heated unraised dough in the sun as they traveled. In memory of this, Jews eat unleavened, or flat, bread during Passover.

This painting shows the Jews escaping from slavery in Egypt by crossing the Red Sea. The Bible tells how God parted the waters for them. After the Jews were safely across, the waters closed in again. The Egyptians who were chasing them drowned.

Today, Jewish people often try to be with their families for Passover. Children journey home to their parents' house. Brothers, sisters, and other relatives travel so that they can be together. Other Jews make a journey to the Western Wall in Jerusalem.

A Jewish family in Jerusalem celebrates the Seder meal together. The man standing up is retelling the story of the Jewish escape from slavery.

The Seder meal

Seder is a special meal eaten on the first two nights of Passover. First, the story of the Jews' escape from Egypt is retold. Then, the meal begins. Special foods are eaten in a particular order. These foods include:

- *matzah*—or unleavened bread
- *maror*—"bitter herbs," which stand for the bitterness of slavery
- *baitzah*—a hard-boiled egg, which stands for the cycle of life
- *zaroah*—a roasted lamb bone
- *haroset*—a mixture of chopped nuts, apples, and wine, to remember the clay used by the Jewish slaves to make bricks
- *karpas*—parsley, lettuce, or other green plants, which stand for the freshness of new life.

Wine is drunk at key moments during the meal. A full cup of wine is also left on the table for the **prophet** Elijah. If he appears to drink his wine, it is a sign that the **Messiah** is coming.

Pilgrimage to Varanasi

On the banks of the Ganges River in northern India sits the city of Varanasi (also called Benares). It is one of the seven **holy** cities of the **Hindu** religion. Ancient writings mention that even 3,000 years ago, Varanasi was a place of learning. The city also appears in the *Mahabharata* (maa-habba-ratta) and the *Ramayana* (ramma-yanna), the two most important pieces of writing in the Hindu religion.

Temples and gods

There are over 1,500 **temples** in Varanasi—one for every 650 people who live there. The temples are popular with **pilgrims,** who go there to worship. Each temple is home to at least one form of god, who appears there as a deity. Each day the god is awakened with bells, purified with incense, bathed, dressed, and fed before going to sleep again that night.

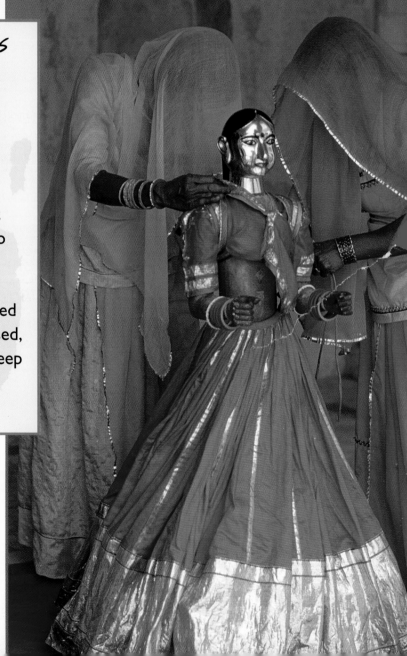

Washing away sin

The Ganges River is holy to Hindus. Each year thousands of Hindus journey to Varanasi to bathe in the river and say prayers. They do this because they believe that bathing in the holy river will wash away their **sins.** The Varanasi *ghats* are very popular. *Ghats* are stone steps used by pilgrims to go down to the water to bathe.

Four out of every five people in India are Hindus. People journey from all over the country to bathe in the Ganges at Varanasi. Some make the **pilgrimage** as hard as possible by crawling part of the way. Many Hindus who live in other countries also make a pilgrimage to Viranasi. Each morning worshippers walk down the *ghats* to bathe in the river.

These Hindus are bathing in the Ganges River.
They hope that the river will clean away their sins.

Sikh Journeys

In the city of Amritsar, in Punjab, a state of northwestern India, there is a lake called Amrit Sarowar. Its name means "the Pool of Immortality." In the middle of the lake is the **holiest** place in the **Sikh** religion—the Harmandir Sahib (Golden Temple). The **temple** is covered in gold leaf (foil).

Many Sikhs and people of other backgrounds visit the Golden Temple each year. There are some handwritten Siri Guru Granth Sahibs (sir-ee goo-roo gran-th sa-hib) in the temple. The Siri Guru Granth Sahib is the **holy** scripture of the Sikh faith. It is stored inside the temple. Although most Sikhs live in Punjab, there are many more living in other countries, and some of them also come to the Golden Temple.

The Golden Temple in Amritsar is the holiest place in the world for Sikhs. Many thousands journey here each year.

Guru Nanak's travels

Today's pilgrims journey by airplane, car, bus, or train. Guru Nanak (1469–1539) made four great journeys that took him all across Punjab and northern India. He tried to combine parts of different religions into one religion that all people could follow equally.

These pilgrims are arriving at the gates of the Golden Temple, where their holy book, the Guru Granth Sahib, is kept.

Nanak and the Brahmins

One day Guru Nanak found himself on the banks of the Ganges River. Standing in the river was a group of Brahmins (Hindu priests). They were throwing water at the sun to quench the souls of their **ancestors.** Nanak waded in and began to throw water in the opposite direction. He told the Brahmins he was watering his fields in the Punjab. They began to mock Nanak until he replied that if their water could reach the sun, his could certainly cover a few hundred miles to Punjab.

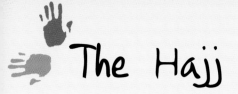

The Hajj

Each year millions of pilgrims journey to the city of Mecca in Saudi Arabia. They are **Muslims,** followers of the Islamic religion. Islam is based on five "pillars," the five duties of all Muslims. One of the five pillars is to visit Mecca if possible. This **pilgrimage** to Mecca is called the *hajj* (haj).

Mecca is the city where Muhammad, the final **prophet** of Islam, was born. It is Islam's most **holy** city. Each year over two million Muslims arrive during the month of pilgrimage. They come from all over the world.

The Great Mosque is at the heart of Islam's holiest city, Mecca.

Worshipping together with so many other Muslims during the hajj is an experience people bring to their own mosques when they return home.

At the heart of the city is the Great **Mosque,** which can hold over a million people. In the courtyard of the mosque is the Kaaba (ka-bah). This word means "a square building" in Arabic. The Kaaba is the most important pilgrim site in Mecca. The Qur'an (kor-AN), the Muslim holy book, says that it was built according to God's plan. Inside is the Black Stone, one of the holiest objects for Muslims. The Black Stone is said to have been given to humans on behalf of God by the angel Gabriel. All Muslims face in the direction of Mecca and the Kaaba five times a day during their prayers.

Jamal's story

Jamal Hussein, thirteen years old, remembers his journey to Mecca:

My father took me to Mecca for the hajj last year. It was amazing—so many people crammed together in such a small space! As we moved from one place to another in a huge crowd, everyone was part of the same thing, all part of our religion together. I hope that one day I can go back and perform the hajj again.

A Journey of Prostration

In the southwestern corner of the Chinese province of Tibet stands Mount Kailash. The mountain is **holy** to **Buddhists,** who believe it is the center of the universe. Each year, many Buddhists visit Mount Kailash, hoping to walk around it. By making the difficult journey around the holy mountain, they believe they gain merit, or **spiritual** reward.

This traveler is clapping his hands together in the first part of a prostration. Repeated again and again as part of a pilgrimage, this tiring way of moving forward is thought to be especially good.

A hard path

The path around the mountain is 32 miles (52 kilometers) long, and it is nearly 3 miles (4.8 kilometers) above sea level. At this height, there is less oxygen in the air. Each breath provides the body with less oxygen, so walkers get tired much faster than they would at sea level. The weather on the mountain is also hard to predict. It is often bitterly cold, windy, and snowy.

To gain extra merit, many Buddhists travel the path while making prostrations. To make prostrations, they clap their hands above their head and move them down their body before falling forward onto their hands and knees. They lie face down on the ground before finally standing up and starting the next prostration. Completing the whole path around Mount Kailash in this way can take several weeks.

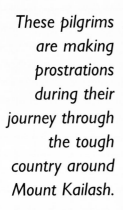

These pilgrims are making prostrations during their journey through the tough country around Mount Kailash.

Dreamtime Wandering

Most Australian Aborigines believe the world was created during the Dreamtime. At that time the **Ancestors,** including a wallaby (small kangaroo) and a crocodile, made themselves out of clay. Aborigines believe that they are each a member of a **clan** started in the Dreamtime by one of the Ancestors.

Some Aborigines can still follow their clan's Songline today.

Ancestral footsteps

As the Ancestors traveled around Australia, they sang out the names of the things and creatures that crossed their paths. By doing so, the Ancestors sang the world into being. At the same time, they scattered behind them trails of words and musical notes that made up a song. These songs were taught to members of their clan and used as a map to follow the path the Ancestor had taken. Since every feature of the landscape was mentioned in the song, it provided a guide to where the Ancestor had walked.

According to Aboriginal beliefs, these song paths crisscross the whole landscape of Australia. Aborigines call them "Footsteps of the Ancestors" or "Way of the Law." Most Europeans know them as "Songlines." Although today many of the songs have been forgotten, some still survive. It is still possible for Aborigines who know the song of their clan to sing their way across the countryside, following the footsteps of their Ancestor.

Songline conflicts

Because the ancient routes of the Songlines are **sacred** to Aboriginal people, they can cause problems between Aborigines and other Australians. Building a new road, for example, could cut a Songline apart, rubbing out the footsteps of the Ancestors and making the path impossible to follow.

Boulders, like this one at the Devil's Marbles in Australia's Northern Territory, can be important markers on a Songline.

Mountain Journeys

Some mountains are climbed for religious reasons—Croagh Patrick in Ireland, for example. Saint Patrick is the patron saint of Ireland. In some **Christian** religions, a patron saint is thought to protect a particular place or activity. According to legend, Saint Patrick stayed on the summit, or highest point, of Croagh Patrick for 40 days without eating. Today, people come from all over the world to climb Croagh Patrick on Reek Sunday (the last Sunday in July). They make this journey to celebrate Saint Patrick's great feat.

This statue of Saint Patrick is on Croagh Patrick in Ireland. Thousands of people climb the mountain on Saint Patrick's Day, some of them barefoot.

Each year hundreds of climbers travel to Mount Everest, in hopes of climbing to its summit. They start here, at the base camp.

People climb other mountains for personal reasons. The journey up the mountain and back is similar to a **pilgrimage** for the people who make it. Each year, thousands of people visit the base of Mount Everest, in the Himalayas. Everest is **sacred** to the Sherpa people, who live in the region. Sherpas act as guides for the tourists who visit Everest. Their name for the mountain is Chomolungma, which means "goddess mother."

To most people, Everest is no more than the world's tallest mountain. Nonetheless, many people have lost their lives trying to climb it. Among them is George Mallory, who never made it back from his attempt to reach the summit in 1924. Other mountaineers have also died during journeys in the Alps, Rockies, Andes, and other mountain ranges around the world.

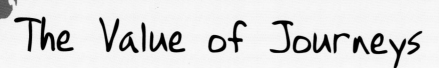

The Value of Journeys

Why do people make the journeys that are described in this book? The English writer Rudyard Kipling once said, "There are two kinds of men in the world—those that stay at home and those that do not." He meant that some people have a need to travel, and others will be sad if they do not.

Climbers on Mont Blanc, France, Europe's highest mountain. Millions of people climb mountains for fun every year.

Animal instinct

Animals' need to travel is even stronger than humans. The scientist Charles Darwin gave the example of Audubon's goose. If its flight feathers are removed, the goose cannot fly on its annual migration (movement to another place to feed or breed). Unable to fly, the goose will walk along the migration path even though it could never finish the journey.

*This picture shows the Kumbh Mela festival in India in January 2001. **Holy** men and women, as well as other **Hindus,** come together to bathe in the Ganges River. The festival takes place every twelve years.*

An ancient Moorish **proverb** says, "He who does not travel does not know the value of men." It means that only by traveling is it possible to find out what people are really like—whether they are kind, cruel, generous, or stingy. Travelers also find out about themselves. During a long walk, many people discover how determined they can be, even when tired. When a fellow traveler has no food or water, people discover how generous they can be even if they are hungry themselves. And most of all, travelers carrying all of their equipment on their back find out how little they really need.

These ideas might explain why traveling is important in most religions. By traveling, religious people realize they need little more than a few possessions and the company of their god.

Glossary

ancestor relative in the past. Your grandparents and great-grandparents are your ancestors.

apostle one of the twelve original followers of Jesus

Buddhist person who follows the way of life taught by Buddha, who lived in ancient India about 2,500 years ago. Buddha was not a god, but a man. He taught his followers how to live simple, peaceful lives—Buddhism.

Christian person who follows the religion of Christianity, which is based on the teachings of Jesus Christ. Christians believe that Jesus was the Son of God.

clan group of people who are all related to one another by birth or marriage

crucified way of killing criminals used by the ancient Romans and others. A criminal was tied to a wooden cross, nails were sometimes driven through the hands and feet, and he or she was left to die.

Hindu person who follows Hinduism. Hindus worship one god (called Brahman) in many forms. Hinduism is the main religion in India.

holy special because it has to do with God or a religious purpose

Jew person who follows the religion of Judaism. Jews pray to one god. Their holy book is the Hebrew Bible, sometimes called the Old Testament by Christians.

mass religious ceremony held by members of the Roman Catholic part of the Christian religion

Messiah person who saves a people who are enslaved; particularly important idea within Judaism

mosque Muslim place of worship

Muslim person who follows the religion of Islam. Muslims pray to one god, whom they call Allah.

New Testament second part of the Christian Bible

pilgrimage journey to a special, often religious, place. A person who goes on a pilgrimage is called a *pilgrim.*

plague great trouble, often some sort of terrible disease from which many people suffer

procession people walking together along a route as part of a public or religious festival

prophet religious teacher, instructed by God

proverb short saying that usually includes a well-known truth

sacred having spiritual or religious importance

Sikh person who follows the religion of Sikhism, based on the teachings of the ten Gurus, or teachers

sin action or thought that is against religious laws. A sinner is someone who commits a sin or sins.

spiritual of the world of the spirit (soul) rather than the physical world

temple place where people worship their religion

treason attempt to overthrow a government or ruler to which the offender owes allegiance

Virgin Mary human mother of Jesus, in Christianity

More Books to Read

Kendall, Sue. *Pilgrimages and Journeys.* Chicago: Raintree, 2001.

Parker, Victoria. *The Golden Temple and Other Sikh Holy Places.* Chicago: Raintree, 2003.

Ross, Mandy. *Mecca.* Chicago: Raintree, 2003.

Ross, Mandy. *The Western Wall and Other Jewish Holy Places.* Chicago: Raintree, 2003.

Index